Thomas Charles
'God's Gift to Wales'

JONATHAN THOMAS

© Day One Publications 2021

ISBN 978-1-84625-703-2

British Library Cataloguing in Publication Data available

Published by Day One Publications
Ryelands Road, Leominster, HR6 8NZ
Telephone 01568 613 740
North America Toll Free 888 329 6630
email—sales@dayone.co.uk
web site—www.dayone.co.uk

Cover design by smallprint

Printed by Cambrian Printers Ltd

For Noah, Levi and Seth
You make me smile
I trust you will know the smile of God in the face of Christ

Contents

List of Illustrations

Series Preface

Mission and Vision: Welsh greats who changed the world for Christ is a series of very readable short biographies of men and women from Wales who have had an amazing influence for good.

Whatever your age or wherever you come from, it is hoped that these real-life stories will inspire you to delve more deeply into their lives. They are meant to excite younger people as well as older readers to take an interest in history and especially in individuals who are so little remembered or even neglected but who have made a significant impact not only in Wales but more generally throughout Britain and beyond.

It is our earnest prayer that the Lord would use these biographical sketches to stimulate, encourage and challenge those who read them to live to the glory of God and the advancement of his kingdom.

Philip H Eveson
Chairman of the Bryntirion Press Committee

Preface

Have you ever met someone who seemed to think just like you? They loved what you were passionate about? Enjoyed what you wanted to spend your time doing? Valued what you cherished? When you find someone like that, you find a true friend. C. S. Lewis said that 'the typical expression of opening friendship would be something like, 'What? You too? I thought I was the only one.'

One summer, as the sun was shining during my holiday in Devon, I made a new friend. I found someone who saw the gospel the same way as I did. In fact, I got to know a guy who was more passionate about the gospel than I was and seemed to love Jesus in a way that inspired me to love the Lord all the more. The odd thing was, this person had been dead for over 200 years! But as I read his letters and sermons it seemed as if he had lived only yesterday. His message was as fresh and relevant as anything I had read or heard in the previous five years.

By now I consider Thomas Charles to be a friend. Every time I read something he has written, I feel like I am sitting with a good mate over a Flat White. So, as good friends shorten each other's names, I'll call him TC in this book. The great thing about my friendship with TC is that he spurs me on to grow in my friendship with God. My hope is that as you read this book you too will share that same passion and burden: to know Jesus more.

As I sat in that sunshine in Devon I read these wonderful words:

> *The rays of heavenly glory, issuing from Christ, pervade the inmost parts of the soul, and convey new vigour to the spiritual life ... It is like looking on the midday sun in a clear summer's day. Our weak eyes are dazzled with its splendour, and unable to look any longer.*

I pray that you may be dazzled.

Jonathan Thomas
Abergavenny, March 2021

Thomas Charles Timeline

1753	Birth of Sally Jones, 12 November
1755	Birth of Thomas Charles, 14 October
1761	Death of Griffith Jones
1769	Enters Carmarthen Academy
1773	Conversion under Rowland's sermon at Llangeitho
1775	Enters Jesus College, Oxford
1778	First meeting with Sally Jones, August
1778-83	Curacies in Somerset
1779	First letter to Sally Jones, 28 December
1780	Ordained priest, 21 May
1782	Calvinistic Methodist chapel at Bala enlarged
1783	Marries Sally, 20 August
1784	Joins Bala Society, 2 July
1784	Birth of Mary Jones, Llanfihangel-y-pennant
1780s	Re-establishes circulating schools
1787	First Sunday school established
1791-93	Revival at Bala
1792	Bala Chapel again enlarged
1799	Left hand frostbitten when crossing Migneint in winter
1800	Mary Jones walks to Bala
1800	Thumb amputated, severe illness, November
1802	Addresses the Religious Tract Society on need for Welsh Bibles
1807	First consignment of the Bible Society's Welsh Bible reaches Bala
1811	Fourth and last part of *Y Geiriadur Ysgrythurol* published
1814	Death of Thomas Charles, 5 October
1814	Death of Sally Charles, 24 October

Introduction

C ome with me on a journey to Wales in the first half of the 1700s. This beautiful land was yet to be scarred by the mining boom, and the industrial revolution of iron making and copper smelting hadn't gained any serious traction. Wales at this time was a small country of less than half a million people who lived mostly by working the land. This usually meant that people were born, lived and died in the same area, often working the same small section of land that their family had for generations before them.

The Church in Wales at this time was not in a great condition. About 200 years earlier, the Protestant Reformation, led by men like Martin Luther on the continent, had arrived in Wales but had not transformed it as had happened in many countries in Europe. A hundred years later, the Puritan Movement had helped start new churches but there had been no great drive to win 'the hearts of the Welsh at large'. The beautiful but sleepy land of Wales was yet to wake up to the power of the gospel.

Plaque on the Charles' house, Bala High Street

While there was a lot of religious activity, like churchgoing and church festival days in the country, there was nothing life-changing. In fact, a book published in 1721 on the state of the church in the diocese of St David's paints a dismal picture of churches turned into barns, uninhabitable vicarages, services conducted at double speed and lingering Roman Catholic superstition.

But just as the industrial revolution was about to catapult Wales into becoming part of the leading nation of the world, a series of revivals broke out. Revivals are spiritual awakenings when large numbers of people in a particular area or country become Christians at about the same time. We will see more of this in chapter 5. These revivals were so powerful that they would send ripples around the earth and, even more, into eternity.

This all began in South Wales with a man called Griffith Jones (1684-1761) from Llanddowror, just outside Carmarthen in south west Wales. Griffith Jones served in the Church of England (the name of the Anglican Church in England and Wales at that time) and started to draw crowds of up to three thousand to hear his preaching. This was not normal. Rather than the double-speed services mentioned in St David's, people were willing to walk double distances just to hear him.

This desire to listen to sermons was unheard of. It may even seem strange to you today! I can still remember sitting through sermons as a boy and counting the bricks behind the preacher's head!

Griffith Jones was a man with great ambitions for the gospel, even hoping to become the first British missionary to India (although he never made it). Locally, he set his sights on starting circulating schools. In those days, you understand, most people didn't go to school and therefore couldn't read or write and because of that they would never be able to read the Bible.

This new system of circulating schools meant that a teacher would arrive at a community and help adults as well as children to learn to read and write, and then move on elsewhere. This would enable more and more people to read. It is estimated that Griffith Jones's schools taught about 200,000, and this was when the population of Wales was only about 450,000!

Griffith Jones's preaching and organizing of schools were not separate activities. They were important aspects of one great vision. The main reason he wanted people to be able to read was so that they could study the Bible for themselves. Without realizing it, Griffith Jones was laying the foundation for a series of great revivals that would sweep the land, as he brought about a situation where large numbers of people could read the Bible in their native Welsh tongue. He would become known as 'the morning star' of the revival.

It was in the year 1735 that the first revival began. A young man called Howell Harris was at a communion service in Talgarth Church, near Brecon. He described in his journal what happened:

At the Table, Christ bleeding on the cross was kept before my eyes constantly; and strength was given me to believe that I was receiving pardon on account of that blood. I lost my burden: I went home leaping for joy.

Around the same time, Daniel Rowland, a young Church of England minister, was listening to Griffith Jones preach in the churchyard at Llanddewi-brefi, Cardiganshire. He also was converted. Two years later, a man from Carmarthenshire called William Williams happened to stop his horse by the wall of Talgarth Church to listen to Howell Harris preaching in the open air. The sermon convinced him that he was a sinner, and soon after he also came to realize that those sins had been forgiven, through faith in Jesus Christ. Together, by God's grace, these three men, Rowland, Harris and Williams, led what has become known as the Methodist Revival, or the Methodist Awakening. This was a mighty movement of God that saw the outpouring of the Holy Spirit across Wales and it was soon experienced across England and Scotland as well. A similar revival took place in America at the same time, where it was known as the Great Awakening. During these years, hundreds of thousands of people were converted. Men and women, boys and girls were completely changed forever.

However, other parts of the country were not affected. There was great hostility to the gospel in many places across Wales. For example, Howell

Harris and some friends were preaching the gospel at Hay-on-Wye in 1740 and were attacked. So severe was the attack that one man later died of his injuries. But it was in North Wales that the opposition was most fierce. When Harris went to Machynlleth, a gun was drawn on him!

In 1741 Harris went to preach the gospel at Bala in the old county of Merioneth. Here he was beaten mercilessly. He did not return to Bala for six years. According to one vicar, the north considered the Methodists to be *'wicked'*! However, during that meeting in Bala when he was beaten, there was a conversion. A young lady by the name of Jane Jones gave her heart to the Lord. Later, she married a man named David who had a shop in Bala and together they had a daughter called Sarah but everyone called her Sally. We shall hear more of her later.

Let's go back to South Wales. In 1773, during this movement of the Spirit, a schoolboy from Carmarthen was converted under the preaching of Daniel Rowland. His name was Thomas Charles. He is commonly known as 'Thomas

Thomas Charles' home in Bala as it is today

Charles of Bala'. Years later, he also would see revival break out under his preaching, and he would help to start an organisation that has contributed to the spread of revivals all over the world to this day.

I am getting ahead of myself! We need to go back to that schoolboy in Carmarthenshire and look at a brief sketch of his life.

Chapter 1: Boyhood

Which would you rather: pick up a book or pick a fight? When I was a boy, it was always a fight. Books were hard to get into, but fights were harder to get out of. If you are boy reading this, well done! I'm not sure I would have read this when I was your age. But, as we are going to see, what you read can have a life-changing effect on you.

Our story begins in a farmhouse called Pant-dwfn situated on the old road between St Clears and Laugharne, in the parish of Llanfihangel Abercywyn, Carmarthenshire. It was a plain-looking dwelling, in a small dip in the land, and was the home of Rice Charles and his wife. Although Rice and his wife may have gone to church regularly, like many people of their day, they didn't really understand the life-transforming message of the gospel.

They were a well-to-do family of five daughters and four sons. TC (Thomas Charles) was the oldest son and was born on October 14, 1755. We know very little about the family home or of the childhood of the children. But we can imagine that it involved playing in the fields, climbing trees, going to the nearby coast to see the sea and castles, and probably making the ten-mile trip to the local town, Carmarthen.

From what we do know, young TC doesn't seem to have had a wild side as a child, but was 'gentle and serious' according to authors of *The Calvinistic Methodist Fathers of Wales*.[1] When a fight broke out, he made sure he didn't get involved. He was, rather, a very studious young man, who loved to read. So, pick a fight or pick up a book? TC would always choose the book. Although, as we will see, later in life he would get into quite a few fights of sorts.

Because of his temperament, his parents wanted him to be a minister in the Church of England. In their view, this would be a good and respectable job for him.

---

1   See *Further Reading* at the end of the book.

So, when he was about twelve, Rice and his wife sent young TC to school at Llanddowror, just down the road. This was one of the schools established by the 'morning star' of the Methodist Revival – Griffith Jones. Griffith had died and gone to glory some five years earlier, and so the two never met. But at this school, TC got more than a good education. You see, the influence of Griffith Jones was still there, meaning that TC was introduced to numerous books written by the Puritan greats.[2] And so he set himself to read as much of the Bible and these blessed books as he could. One of the books that really struck him at the time was John Bunyan's *The Doctrine of the Law and Grace Unfolded*.

During this time he began to be troubled because of his spiritual state. This means he started to worry about where he stood with God. While he had been a good boy in many ways, he was bothered by the question: 'Am I good enough for God?' To try and find the answer he would go to hear as much preaching as possible. So seriously did he take this pursuit, that he introduced family worship in the home. But it seems that the spiritual temperature of the locality was very cold indeed. While Griffith Jones's influence remained, it had waned. TC writes in his journal: *I had not one spiritual person to speak to for some time.* This was at school in Llanddowror!

Yet, by God's grace, he found a spiritual mentor in an old disciple of Griffith Jones, a man called Rees Hugh. Although Rees was a much older man, they would meet a couple of times a week to discuss spiritual matters. Rees wasn't a reader like TC, and lived a life of poverty. There was nothing special or significant about him, except for one thing: his knowledge of God and of the Bible. Years later, TC called him his 'Father in Christ'. Their conversations would never leave TC unaffected.

TC was starting to see something of the heart-felt nature of the gospel, how God could change a person from within. But he wasn't a Christian yet. He describes his spiritual state at the time:

---

2   The Puritans were Protestant Christians from the 16th and 17th centuries who did not believe that the Anglican Church had gone far enough in reforming from its Roman Catholic background. They wanted to continue to grow the Church in purity both theologically and practically. They had a deep sense of God.

My religion consisted principally in earnest longings and strong desires after something which I had not hitherto obtained; together with a determined resolution to continue to use all appointed means to find it.

At the tender age of fourteen, TC left his family home and went to study at the academy in nearby Carmarthen. Ten miles doesn't seem much today, but in those days it would have been a different world – a world full of new experiences and influences. What would happen to him here? With freedom from home and new temptations from the big town, what was to become of young TC?

Both he and Rees Hugh prayed fervently that he would not fall to temptation or be side-tracked from the things of God. It could easily have happened. TC writes of nearly being *ruined by a set of careless, high spirited, jolly professors.* The big question was: how would TC free himself from these influences?

Part of the answer was for him to become a member of the local Methodist society. As we know, the Methodist Revival impacted the area and changed thousands of lives. Many of the people who had experienced the truly life-transforming power of the gospel had not been able to remain within the local parish churches, and so they had set up Methodist societies. In these societies people would share details of their spiritual state and experiences, and a vibrancy of faith was clearly evident. It wasn't the sort of place where you would just sit and count the bricks behind the preacher's head! It was a place to become spellbound.

In going to the Methodists, TC was surrounded by men and women who had true heart-felt faith. Some of the men helped him grasp more of the glorious gospel and, as he had started in Llanddowror, he continued reading many great books. TC filled his mind with the gospel. He searched the Scriptures and sought the Lord. He was looking for God. Finally, just like arriving at a beautiful destination after a long and winding journey, TC was converted. He was eighteen years old.

He wrote a wonderful description of his experience of conversion. It happened when he went to hear the great preacher, Daniel Rowland, a leader of the Methodist movement. It was so life-changing that TC said that becoming a Christian was better than the blind receiving sight! Here is the story in his own words:

> *January 20, 1773, I went to hear Mr Rowland preach at New Chapel; his text was Hebrews 4:15. A day much to be remembered by me as long as I live. Ever since the happy day I have lived in a new heaven and a new earth. The change a blind man who receives his sight experiences does not exceed the change I at that time experienced in my mind...*
>
> *Then I was first convinced of the sin of unbelief or entertaining narrow, contracted and hard thoughts of the Almighty. I had such a view of Christ as our High Priest, of his love, compassion, power, and all-sufficiency, as filled my soul with astonishment — with joy unspeakable and full of glory. My mind was overwhelmed and overpowered with amazement. The truths exhibited to my view appeared too wonderfully gracious to be believed. I could not believe for very joy. The glorious scenes then opened to my eyes will abundantly satisfy my soul millions of years hence in the contemplation of them...*
>
> *Often in walking in the fields I looked up to heaven with joy and called that my home, at the same time ardently longing for the appearance of the glorious Saviour to take me forever to himself.*

Listen to what he writes:

> *The effect of this sermon remained on my mind above half a year, during which time I was generally in a comfortable and heavenly frame.*

Wow! Have you ever had an experience like that? The amazing thing is, this is possible for everyone. Even you!

TC soon felt called by God to enter the ministry and so, in 1776 he went on to continue his education at Jesus College, Oxford. He was 20 years old and set out on the longest journey of his life – and he probably walked there! Although his family was prosperous compared to many of their neighbours, they were not rich. They could only afford to send one son to university. And it wasn't all plain sailing when he arrived.

TC wrote of a time, while at Oxford, when he ran out of money. He had nothing except debts to pay. What would he do? He couldn't skype home and ask for a money transfer or a student loan. There was no way to get the money or so it seemed. He found that his faith grew as he had to trust completely in the Lord. Then he had a most amazing and formative experience.

Miles from home, with no hope of being bailed out, and with a £20 debt to the college, which would have been about £1,500 in today's money, he flung himself on the Lord's mercy. He must have prayed and prayed. And then something happened, something completely unexpected. He wrote:

> *a gentleman sent for me to dine with him; I went, and before we parted, to my great surprise, he produced the twenty pound note I wanted, and at the same time told me that I should not want during my stay at Oxford.*

What an amazing God! This experience of God's goodness would set him up for his future ministry and life. Did you see what the man said? Not only did he pay the £20 debt, he also offered to take care of him for the rest of his studies!

In the summer of 1797 TC went to Olney, in Buckinghamshire, to be an intern with John Newton, the converted slave-ship captain who wrote the hymn 'Amazing grace'. This was a great opportunity and it turned out to be a time of growth in his faith and in his understanding of what it meant to be a minister. TC and John Newton got on so well during that summer internship that it proved to be the beginning of a long and close friendship.

TC wrote about his time there:

Having a Newton to be instructed by, both by edifying discourses in the pulpit, and by conversation in the closet, what place or situation can I be in, more pleasing and delightful?

It must have been a glorious summer. During that placement he learnt a key lesson that never left him:

One may speak a great deal, and that very orthodox, but unless he has a little of the unction of the Holy Spirit, he might, for aught I know, as well be silent. This is what I want in my prayers, studies, and meditations.

The following summer, 1778, having finished his studies, he went to Bala on a walking-tour with his college friend, Simon Lloyd. Bala is surrounded by beautiful mountains and hills and, on the edge of the town, there is a picturesque lake that captivates your gaze. This would have been the perfect place to relax and recoup after the years of study in Oxford. But there was more. TC saw something greater than the beautiful hills and captivating lake.

Simon Lloyd

TC met a beautiful girl who would captivate his heart. This would change his life. He met, and fell for, Sally Jones. This was the daughter of the shopkeeper converted when Howell Harris was beaten up all those years ago, the one we met earlier in the introductory chapter. But there was no whirlwind romance. Nothing happened, and nothing would really happen for some time.

On that same trip to Wales, TC preached what was probably his first sermon, at his home parish church in Carmarthenshire. His 'father in Christ', Rees Hugh, was there, and TC shares: *I could almost have cried with joy*. He had come home a changed man, ready to serve the Lord and preach the gospel and his old friend had been there to see it. A few weeks later, Rees Hugh went to be with the Lord.

Immediately afterwards, TC was ordained as a deacon in Oxford, and then began his curacy, the first step to becoming a minister, in Shepton Beauchamp in Somerset. It did not go well. While solidly a Church of England man, TC had what would be considered a Methodist mindset.

You will remember that we saw that the Established Church was not very healthy in Wales. Things were a little better in England but that didn't mean that every church in the land wanted to hear the life-transforming message of the gospel. Many churches disapproved of the heart-felt, serious and biblical preaching that characterised the Methodist preachers.

The sermons that TC preached would be described as evangelical today. That is, they focused on the teaching of the Bible that everyone must put their trust in the work of Jesus on the cross for salvation. Good works were not good enough. Religious duties were not good enough. The only thing that could save was faith in Jesus and such a change would be complete, from the inside out. So when TC started preaching this message, this very Methodist message, persecution began. People didn't just sit back and count the bricks, they thought about throwing bricks!

He was in a desperate situation, but he knew the goodness of God even there. He described the experience like this: *Providence at present appears dark ... At present I have no friend but the Lord Almighty.* He was in a similar position to Paul when he wrote his second letter to Timothy. Yet, even though he was offered a way to escape to another parish, he chose to remain. TC was turning out to be a strong man. He wasn't just going to give up.

Yet, in fact, it was not really his decision. His boss, the vicar of the parish, did not want him around either, but, instead of firing him, he just reduced his wages. Once again TC had to struggle for money. It simply wasn't enough to live on. There was no way he could survive on the small wages he was given.

Therefore, in 1780, he took on further work in the parish of Milbourne Port, also in Somerset, where he could serve under an evangelical clergyman.

He must have felt like a bird released from a cage. He could now preach the gospel and enjoy fellowship with a fellow Christian. In the same year, he was raised from the position of deacon to that of a minister able to preside at the communion table. TC was growing in faith and ministry, but he knew he still had a long way to go. He wrote in his journal: *Endow me with a double portion of thy Spirit and clothe me with power from on high.*

TC spent four years working in that church and was happy enough. But his heart was elsewhere.

The church at Milbourne Port, Somerset

Chapter 2: Bala

We're back again to Sally behind the shop-counter in Bala! It seems that TC had heard about Sally even before he visited Bala. She had a wonderful reputation that had spread as far as Carmarthen. So, when TC went to that beautiful lakeside town, he was already on the lookout. One look is all it took, a life-transforming look!

But, just as there was no whirlwind romance that summer, there was nothing rapid at all. In fact, after he left, TC took until the end of the following year, around sixteen months later, to pluck up the courage even to write his first letter to her. It is well worth reading highlights from the first two letters. These might turn out to be some of the best letters you ever read.

Queen Camel, December 28, 1779

My very dear friend,

Such an unexpected address from a person who never saw you but once, and that at such a long interval of time, will I suppose at first not a little surprise you…

I assure you that long as the interval is since I had the pleasure of seeing you, you have not been absent from my mind for a whole day, from that time to this.

The first report of your character (which I heard at Carmarthen by some of our religious friends about six years ago) left such an impression on my mind as, I am sure, no length of time can ever obliterate. I immediately conceived an ardent desire, and a secret hope, that my Heavenly Father's wise and good Providence would so order subsequent events that I should in due time see that beloved person of whom I had formed such a favourable opinion.

When Mr. Lloyd gave me a kind invitation to spend part of the summer with him at Bala, 'tis inexpressible what secret pleasure and joy the prospect of seeing you afforded me. Nor was I disappointed. The sight of so much good sense, beauty and unaffected modesty, joined with that genuine piety which eminently adorns your person, administered fuel to the fire already enkindled, and which has continued burning with increasing ardour from that time to this…

…Be perfectly assured that nothing but real regard and sincere affection for your person only could ever induce me to write or speak to you on such a subject. You are the only person that ever I saw (and the first I ever addressed on the subject), with whom I thought I could spend my life in happy union and felicity, and for whom I possessed that particular affection and esteem requisite for conjugal happiness; and you are the only temporal blessing I have for some time past asked with importunity of the Lord. I hope that your determination will happily convince me that the Lord's answer is favourable…

I hope to commit this, as well as all other events to him, who rules supremely in the whole universe, and orders all things in the best manner for the advancement of his own glory, and the eternal welfare of his people, and no doubt will order this even for our mutual happiness. To whose mercy and protection I shall not fail to recommend you by constant prayers, and intercessions for you, which are never more ardent and sincere than when you are interested in them.

I shall anxiously wait for a letter from you. I hope it will be favourable. Communicate your thoughts with freedom, and without the least reserve, for you may depend with unshaken confidence upon the most inviolable secrecy from me…

Your most unfeigned friend and humble servant,

Thomas Charles

He didn't hold back! So, how did Sally respond to such a gushing and loving letter? Well, not as you might expect. She finds it all a little strange, which, I guess, you would too.

Bala, January 17, 1780

Reverend Sir,

Your letter doth indeed seem something strange to me. I can neither give it full credit nor throw it aside heedless. May he who knoweth your motive in writing, give me simplicity to answer and let the consequence be what it will.

The liberty and privilege of my present state are very dear and valuable to me. I often wish I had no temptation to part with them; but I can't say I have ever determined or known the will of God concerning it. I trust his providence will in time make this clear. I have several reasons that I do not choose to engage in a correspondence of this nature. But if any letters be exchanged between us I would wish each of us should have free liberty to drop the correspondence at pleasure.

Probably after receiving this you will not wish to write again. This will be no disappointment to me. I quit my claim of every profession in your letter excepting one, which is the remembrance of me at the throne of mercy. This is a pleasing thought which I am willing to cherish, and though I do not expect to see you in this vale of troubles, yet I shall meet you where I hope my gratitude will be in full perfection, there to express it to the glory of him that heareth the prayer of his people for one another and blesses them in the remotest part of the earth.

I have by your permission shown your letter to my father. He and my mother join in cordial respects and love to you. I believe my poor father is an Israelite indeed in whom there is no guile. He, dearest of mortals, thinks everything sincere. I join with him in best wishes for your prosperity in the glorious and very weighty work you are engaged,

Who am your well-wisher,

Sally Jones

What is going on? I think the Welsh literature scholar, Wyn James, is right when he comments, 'she rather suspected TC of having his eye on her money.' Was TC just looking for someone to give financial support toward his ministry? Not at all! But he would have to prove that this was the case.

How would you feel if you were TC reading that letter? Would you give up? Well, he was not one to give up so easily, and he knew that Sally was a young woman of good character. She had been right to respond the way she did … and to tell her father! If anything, this odd response confirmed in him what a wonderful woman she was! So began a series of letters in which their love and affection began, slowly but steadily, to grow.

His letters were full of dreams and hopes, whilst hers were often dry and factual. His would start with phrases like 'My sweet love' and 'my dear, dearest heart'. She would start with 'Reverend Sir.' Ouch! Even the length of the letters was different. At one point, TC begs her to write longer letters. Yet, they keep corresponding.

Throughout the letters they spend time writing of the sufficiency of Christ and of how all of our true happiness is found only in him. In one letter TC writes that, *there can be no happiness but in the enjoyment of the inexhaustible and overflowing source of all goodness and perfection.*

They understood that their relationship could never be the basis of their happiness. However, they also agreed that God, in his goodness, has designed that *creatures of God can, and do, contribute much to our happiness.* Getting that right was vital for TC and Sally, and it is vital for you too.

For their love to blossom, TC would have to move to Bala. There was no way that Sally would leave to be with him. As an only child, who loved being close to her parents, she simply could not consider leaving. TC put it like this: *I found that it would be worse than death for her to be removed.* So, he had to come back to Wales, to Bala. But Wales was already in his heart, so this was the natural thing to do. He just needed a church.

John Newton wrote to say that he could obtain a place for him in a church in the Vale of Glamorgan, but this was too far away from Sally. Newton's influence did not spread much further, and he could not find any parishes for him in North Wales. So, without any income, TC moved anyway! In 1783, five years after he had walked the mountains and been captivated by young Sally, they were married on the edge of Bala Lake at Llanycil. TC had arrived in Bala!

During his life in this little town, TC faced numerous attacks from many places. Early on, he faced an internal struggle involving his relationship with the Church of England and with Methodism. It is hard for us to understand how important and defining it was to be associated with the Methodists in those days.

Llanycil Church, Bala, where Thomas and Sally were married and where they are buried

While the Methodist societies or fellowship meetings had been growing, they were still not an official church and were seen as a renegade movement that would eventually fade away. They were trying to work within the

Established Church but this was awkward and difficult. As we have seen, the relationship between them was not good. While TC was a Methodist in terms of the gospel and preaching, he was still happy to be a minister of the Church of England. He had no plan to leave. He wanted to stay and preach the gospel.

Before he arrived in Bala, it seemed that he had found a curacy in Oswestry, Shropshire, which was the closest he could get. But he wrote: *The moment the Vicar heard that I was tinctured with what they call Methodistical principles, he would have nothing more to say to me.* Other possibilities of curacies came and went, but people did not want to appoint him. His Methodism was too much. He talked too much about things like sin, grace and the need to trust in Jesus.

Thankfully, Sally was a good business woman and the small shop in Bala was able to support them both. The financial burden of being without an income for TC did not affect them. Yet, TC continued to believe that he was called to the Church of England. So, while waiting for a solution, he was willing to travel fifty miles into England, to the village of Shawbury, seven miles from Shrewsbury, to work with an evangelical vicar there.

But that wasn't going to work in the long run. Undeterred, he tried another church in a place called Llangynog. But he only lasted two Sundays! Listen to what happened:

> *Last Sunday, the whole parish with 2 or 3 of the principal inhabitants at their head came to me and accosted me in a rougher strain than I ever have been used to before. They insisted on my preaching no more in their church, for they added, you have cursed us enough already.*

He was next appointed to a church in Llanymawddwy, a little Welsh village about fourteen miles south of Bala. Those fourteen miles were over a mountain that my car struggles to get up even today! Yet, he would cross that mountain, twice a week, even in the freezing snow.

His work was blessed in Llanymawddwy as people were affected by his preaching. God was working through him, changing lives. But even this fruitful ministry was short-lived because the usual opposition soon broke out. The powers-that-be were happy to get rid of him by making all kinds of accusations against him.

Sadly, the rector of the church simply listened to the accusations and accepted them, writing to tell TC to leave immediately. No questions were asked. What an injustice! But then it got worse. When the local people heard this, they organised a petition to keep him but it was highjacked before it could be handed in! TC complained to the Bishop, but he was ignored.

I wonder how you would feel if something like that happened to you? TC wrote a letter to his *dear Sally* explaining the situation. It included the following line, *I am happy in the Lord. Pray for me, and in the midst of everything rejoice in the Lord.* Just as the truths they had discussed and agreed on in their letters about happiness in Christ coming before relationships, so also happiness in Christ came before acceptance in the ministry. This was a lesson that TC had learnt in England and it would serve him well over the years to come. It was also something that Sally would remind him of many times in future years.

The uncertainty was causing him much internal turmoil. What was going on? What should he do? He turned to friends for advice. John Newton got to hear that he was questioning whether or not to preach in the Methodist societies. Newton's answer was straight and simple: he should leave Bala, and even Wales, if necessary, and settle in whatever place he could find where an Established Parish Church would have him. This was tough. What was he to do?

One thing we can say for certain about TC is that he was determined, even when in great difficulty. Listen to what he wrote at this time: *I feel myself much inclined to take Wales, as I did my wife, for better, for worse, till death do us part.* If he had to choose between the Established Church and Wales, it seems that Wales would win.

While he himself never wished to leave the Church of England, it seems that a dream sealed the deal. It was a terrifying dream of the Last Day, the Judgment Day. When he awoke, he asked himself what answer he could give if, on that Day, Jesus, the Judge, questioned him: *Why standest thou here idle?* Is that what he was doing? Standing idle behind the counter in Bala, when he should be behind the pulpit?

He knew what he had to do. He had to leave the Church and use his gifts and talents in the Methodist cause. So, in 1784, he started attending the local Methodist society and in the summer of that year he joined their ranks. Gone was the security and the status that the Established Church could offer; gone the money, the house, the respect.

Early 19th century print of the Charles' shop and home

As an old man, in 1810, he reflected:

I am so much gladder that I have spent the last 23 years of my life as I have, wandering up and down our cold and barren land, than if I had been made an archbishop ... It was no choice of my own; Providence led me.

TC was the first clergyman in North Wales to move over to Methodism, and when Daniel Rowland heard him preach in Llangeitho in 1785, he said that he was *the gift of God to North Wales*. The Church of England, in Wales at least, didn't take this too well, and there were many attacks and slanders over the years. For example, the Bishop of St Asaph sent him legal warnings and threatened him with imprisonment. But, it must be remembered that he had good friends within the Established Church in England and these were able to obtain help for him from other powerful and influential contacts.

Many years later, another great battle of conscience would arise over the ordination of Methodist preachers, which would have the immediate effect of making the Methodist Church in Wales a separate Christian denomination. This was to be a controversial decision that involved a painful, but principled, change of mind for TC. Not only did he remove his objection to the ordination, a step that meant that the Methodist preachers would be able to serve communion to the societies, but he was also willing to write the manual for communion services for them. Also, after the decision had been taken by the Methodist body, he was to rebuke firmly those who would not respect the majority view.

As well as the ministerial responsibilities that TC shouldered at Bala, he was consistently involved in writing and printing. His first book was a short catechism for children, written in 1791. This is a little book filled with questions and answers to help children understand the Christian faith. It went through many re-prints. In its first ten years over 320,000 copies were sold!

In 1799 he started a magazine called *Trysorfa Ysprydol* (*The Spiritual Treasury*) with some friends, chief of whom was his closest colleague, Thomas

Jones, Denbigh. This became *Y Drysorfa* (*The Treasury*) after the first 6 issues but ended in 1813. Interestingly, this was, as Gwyn Davies says, 'the first Welsh Christian magazine'. He also wrote a response to a book attacking the Methodists, written by an Anglesey clergyman, the Rev T. E. Owen.

But, the big book, his greatest literary achievement, arrived in the early 1800s, when he wrote his *Geiriadur Ysgrythurol* (*A Bible Dictionary*). This started off as a group project, but very soon TC took over all responsibility. It was published in 4 volumes! This work absolutely transformed the pulpits of Wales. It raised the theological bar and is still found on many shelves in Wales today.

It is fair to say that TC did not stand idle. But that said, I still haven't really told you the main things that TC did in Bala. He did more, a lot more.

Chapter 3: Bibles

How do you feel about a snowy day? I love them. The schools close and everything stops. As a boy I relished any excuse to miss lessons and climb a local hill in my winter clothes to enjoy my home-made bobsleigh. For many of us, missing school seems a treat, and walking through snowy mountains a joy. But in TC's day it was quite the opposite. For most children there were no schools to go to, though they would have loved to do so. This was especially true in North Wales.

Take for example, Jacob Jones. He was a weaver who lived in a little cottage at the foot of Cader Idris, twenty-five miles from Bala. Cader is a beautiful mountain that always looks impressive, whatever the weather. Today, many people drive to a car park just down the road, put on their walking boots, and trek to the summit on a sunny day.

But in the 1700s people would have to walk on those stony roads and mountain paths just to get to a neighbour's house or a shop. Buying food, seeing friends and going to church were all difficult and, at times, dangerous things to do. Journeys of many miles for everyday things were commonplace.

During the dark evenings of winter, Jacob's wife would often get her daughter, Mary, to carry a lamp for her on her journey to the local Methodist society. Children like Mary would never get an opportunity to go to school, to learn to read and write or to own a Bible to read.

Having moved to Bala, and learnt of these kinds of difficulties at first hand, TC could see clearly the great need. His heart ached because he wanted people to get into the Bible as he had, because he believed that it alone contained the words of life. The message of the Bible had changed his entire life and he wanted everyone to have that experience.

As TC saw it, there were three barriers to this being fulfilled: first, most people couldn't read; then, too few people knew what the Bible was about; and finally, the vast majority of families didn't own Bibles. One historian has written: 'He found that there was scarcely a neighbourhood in which one out of every twenty of the population could read the Word of God, while there were some localities in which it was difficult to find a single person who was able to do so'. So TC set about removing all these barriers, starting with the pattern he had experienced for himself in Llanddowror.

Circulating Schools

As a boy, TC had learnt to read and write in a school started by Griffith Jones, who, as we saw in a previous chapter, was the founder of the Circulating Schools Movement. These had been really effective in South Wales in helping community after community to ensure that their people became literate. However, these circulating schools had never made much of an impact in the north. TC brought to the north what Griffith Jones had begun over twenty-five years earlier in the south. He arranged his first circulating school in 1785.

The way it worked was simple. A teacher would arrive in a village or town and stay for six to nine months in order to teach the children in the daytime and adults at night how to read and write. Then, he would move on; he would circulate. Amazingly, in that short time a good foundation was laid. The teaching was done entirely through the medium of Welsh, as that was the only language spoken by the vast majority at the time. TC believed that it was quicker and more effective to learn to read first of all in your mother tongue.

In an article he wrote about the schools, he estimated that to teach the children to read English first, before Welsh, would take over two years. It was easier to teach people in a language they already understood and loved; it was their heart language. Having learnt to read Welsh, it was so much easier, if you so desired, to learn to read English afterwards. But he was also certain that by teaching the children to read Welsh first he was demonstrating to them that he was more concerned for their souls than for anything else. In other words, he wasn't just intent on them learning in order to get a better job. He was interested in their hearts, not their careers. The first thing necessary, therefore, was that they should read the Bible in their own language.

He started with one teacher and twenty years later in 1794, he had twenty teachers circulating throughout North Wales! This is an amazing achievement. There was no government funding and, unlike Griffith Jones's work, there was no Church support. So how could he afford to run this extensive organisation? He paid for it in three ways: from any money that he received when preaching at his own society at Bala, or at the other societies which he served; from any profits that his amazing wife could spare from the shop; and from subscriptions from generous supporters across the border in England.

It is worth pausing here to think about the second of those three avenues of support: 'profits that his amazing wife could spare from the shop'. In many ways, Sally is the silent hero in this story. But for her, TC would not have been able to do what he did. It was TC's own testimony that *the support for himself and his family rested upon Mrs Charles's labours in the shop.* She was an exceptional tradeswoman. This worthy woman deserves more attention than she has received. It was only by means of her energetic efforts and her shouldering of such widespread responsibilities that her husband's hands were free for the work of the gospel. The work that Sally freed TC to do was eternal in its impact. Listen to TC describe what happened through the schools:

> *Whatever we attempted of this nature succeeded wonderfully; till the whole country was filled with schools of one sort or another; and all were taught at once. The blessed effects were corresponding; a general concern for eternal things took place in many large districts; many hundreds were awakened to a sense of sin, and their need of Christ, and I have every reason to believe are now faithful followers of him.*
>
> *The schools are still carried on, and the effects the same in a greater or less degree; the number of teachers increase or diminish, as my finances will allow; all my income from a chapel which I serve, I devote wholly towards their support, being supported myself by the industry of my wife.*

> *I visit the schools myself, and catechise them publicly; I have the*
> *unspeakable satisfaction of seeing the general aspect of the country*
> *most amazingly changed; to see the wilderness blossom, as the rose,*
> *and the thirsty land, become springs of water; through the schools,*
> *and the preaching of the Gospel, the spread of divine knowledge is*
> *become universal. Bless the Lord, O my soul!*

So problem one was solved: people could read. But in solving the problem of illiteracy by means of the schools, TC had only begun to tackle the true need: the increasing hunger for spiritual things arising in the hearts of the many thousands of converts of the Methodist Awakening.

Sunday Schools

In the mid 1780s TC started Sabbath schools, that we call Sunday schools. These were not little classes held during a morning church service where children get to colour-in and eat Haribos. These were separate sessions on a Sunday, when young and old would come to study the Bible at a deep level.

Robert Raikes had started a similar system in England four years before, but his organization was only for children. TC created a system in Wales that was unique, in that these Sunday Schools were for all ages, from young children learning their ABC to old people in their eighties and nineties reading words of Scripture for the first time. One author has claimed that they proved to be 'one of the most important and efficient means of grace in the Principality.'

Surprisingly, the Sunday Schools faced opposition even from the Church. People thought that the schools involved doing work on the Sabbath. Towns such as Penrhyndeudraeth and Dolgellau were opposed to them. TC had to think of creative ways of holding them. One Sunday school resorted to meeting at 6am! Interestingly, the opposition didn't just come from the Established Church. Dr Lewis Edwards commented: 'He suffered moral martyrdom for long years, and at the hands of his friends. But on he proceeded, quietly and busily, with no fuss and bother. There was a life that would not die in the Sunday Schools'.

Here is his description of the Sabbath schools in 1806:

It has been my delightful work, since I left London in December last, every Sunday to catechise publicly, and hear them repeat chapters before thousands of people ... In order to give you some idea of the work, I would just mention some of the following particulars, which are strictly true:

Whole families, young and old, the governors and the governed, learn the Catechisms together, and chapters of the Bible; they have appeared together, and repeated alternately what they have learnt. All the grown-up young people, in some of our Societies, have done the same.

Boys and Girls, from eight to sixteen years old, learn whole books of the Scripture; and repeat what time will permit us to hear, such as the whole epistle to the Ephesians, Hebrews, etc; others learn select chapters to an astonishing number, such as 10, 20, 30.

One little girl learnt seventy-two psalms and chapters; and another the astonishing number of ninety-two, the list of which I have in my possession. Now, we want to feed this fire, so happily kindled in their minds, by putting into their hands a few useful Tracts in the Welsh language.

Wow! Did you read that?! These children had learnt to read and then went on to memorize thirty chapters of the Bible! Not thirty verses but thirty chapters! I actually own a book which has the inscription 'Presented on the memorization of the Book of Proverbs'. That wasn't presented to me. As a child in my Sunday school I only ever managed one memory verse in Welsh, and only three words of it: 'Duw cariad yw' ('God is love'). But it is an amazing verse.

We need to note the link here. The Sunday Schools would not have been possible without the Circulating Schools. The Circulating Schools provided the Sunday School teachers. There were not enough people around who could read the Bible in order to teach it. The Circulating Schools changed all that by producing an army of teachers for the Sunday Schools. This was all part of the plan. TC was a great organiser and strategic thinker when it came to the work of the gospel.

Catechisms

One particular aspect of the Sunday Schools that is worth mentioning is the use of catechisms. We mentioned in the last chapter that TC wrote and published a really popular one for children. This was the most important catechism that he wrote and developed, but there were also smaller catechisms written in response to particular, or local, moral dangers. For example, once, when a famous annual fair was expected at a locality, TC wrote a catechism on the evils of dancing.

The question and answer went like this: *Is dancing a sin, my children? Yes, because of the dancing of Herodias's daughter, the head of John the Baptist was cut off.* The children learnt the catechism and recited it publicly before their parents and neighbours and it had great effect. People didn't dance. People didn't get drunk. And the poor fairground harpists had to leave early. So popular were these catechisms that they led to Schools' Festivals, where people would come together to hear the questions and answers in public. These would become regular events in some communities, continuing for many years, even into the second half of the twentieth century.

Two problems were now being solved. The children could read, and they knew parts of the Bible. But as the children and the adults came to know the Bible, they began to develop a spiritual hunger. TC was good at problem-solving, even if this led to more problems. This latest solution of helping people to memorize the Scriptures and grow in spiritual hunger had led to another, glorious, complication: people needed their own Bibles!

The Bible Society

Let's go back to the small cottage at the foot of Cader Idris where Jacob's little daughter, Mary, benefited from all this. When she was ten years old, a Circulating School and Sunday School started two miles down the road. She committed herself wholeheartedly to the schools and became well known for the way she could memorize parts of the Bible. But, like many others in the same situation, while she loved the Bible and knew how to read it, she didn't own one. The closest Bible to Mary was in a farmhouse two miles away. For six years she would walk there every week to read it.

There was a famine of Bibles in the land. This had been a problem for a long time. Griffith Jones had arranged for an organisation called the SPCK (The Society for the Promotion of Christian Knowledge) to produce two editions of the Welsh Bible (1746 and 1752). But these were mainly sold in South Wales. Later, Peter Williams published a Welsh Bible, but it cost too much for the peasant people to afford. So, in 1787, TC started writing to friends in England for help to get more Welsh Bibles printed.

Help from the SPCK was always going to be very difficult as they were a Church of England Society, and TC had turned his back on them. In 1792, by God's grace, he heard that the SPCK were intending to publish a Welsh Bible of their own accord. But a year later they changed their minds, saying that they did not believe there was any need for it in Wales! As we know, TC was not one to give up. Onwards he battled. Eventually, in 1799, after much effort and perseverance, he obtained 10,000 Bibles and 2,000 New Testaments from the SPCK. These sold out straight away! Of course there was a need. He went back to them, asking for a further supply but the SPCK would not reprint again. The need in Wales was as desperate as ever.

It was about this time that Mary Jones, now fifteen years of age, decided to walk the twenty-five miles from her home at the foot of Cader Idris, over that great mountain, to find TC in Bala and buy one of the Bibles. She didn't know that he had sold them all. For the last six years she had been saving every penny to buy a Bible and she finally had enough. Sometime in 1800, she set out on stony roads and mountain tracks, keeping her shoes in her bag so as not to wear them out. Arriving late in the evening, she found a place to sleep at a local preacher's house. The next morning she went to call on TC and with her shoes on, of course.

With great excitement she knocked at the door of his house and asked to see Mr Thomas Charles. Holding the money she had saved for six years, she asked to buy a Bible, a Bible just like the one she had walked two miles to read and relish every week. This was the biggest moment of her life. She would finally be able to read the Bible every day. Then came the crushing news: TC had sold all his Bibles. He did not have one to give her. Her journey had been a waste. She would have to go home empty-handed. They both wept.

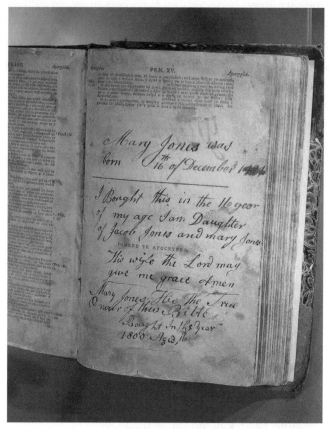

Mary Jones's Bible

But the story didn't end there. TC had a small number of Bibles kept to one side, promised for some friends. His heart melted, and he sold her one of these. Her tears of desperation turned to tears of delight. TC said to a friend who was with him at the time: *Isn't that a sight to melt the hardest heart – an intelligent, poor girl, walking barefoot fifty miles, in coming and going, to obtain a Bible? I must not now rest until I find a way to fill the country with God's Word.* Little Mary Jones had started something that would change the world.

Over the next two years, TC spoke to a group of friends whom he used to meet in London. His purpose was to solve a Welsh problem, but the result would be the solving of a world-wide problem. He shared with the men the story of Mary Jones, and it is still shared to this day in schools up and down Wales, and throughout the world, and yet again, many tears were shed. The burden was shared and the passion was spread. A Baptist minister, Joseph Hughes, cried out: *And if for Wales, why not also for the Empire and for the world?* And so, by 1804, the British and Foreign Bible Society (BFBS) was officially launched,[3] with the slogan: 'Beibl i bawb o bobl y byd!' ('A Bible for all the people of the world'). Not only Welsh Bibles were needed, innumerable groups of people all over the world needed Bibles in their own language.

Wonderfully, in 1806, the first batch of these new BFBS Welsh Bibles reached Wales, and to Bala first of all. The scene was remarkable. People ran out into Bala High Street as they heard that the cart was approaching the town. Cheers rang out and prayers were offered as the load of Bibles arrived to satisfy the hunger of a nation. By God's amazing grace, 20,000 Bibles and 5,000 New Testaments were delivered. Within 10 years the Bible Society had supplied 100,000 copies!

But, all was not plain sailing, as we have seen, and there were plenty more battles ahead.

---

3   Today, it is just called 'The Bible Society' and produces millions of copies of the Scriptures every year in scores of different languages.

Chapter 4: Battles

Have you ever had rocks thrown at you? No? I once got into a snowball fight that ended badly because someone had not realised there were little stones in their wintry bullets. Even a little bit of grit in a friendly play fight can hurt. But what about having rocks thrown at you, with full force? That must be terrifying and that happened to TC as he continued spreading the message of the gospel in other areas of North Wales.

We have already seen how TC had to deal with the internal struggle of leaving the Church of England and getting involved with Methodism. We have also looked at how he had to fight to get Sunday Schools launched and Bibles printed. It seems that everything he did had to be fought for. But we haven't seen signs of physical fights yet. Most of his battles were conducted by the pen or through the Press.

Having gone into Methodism, which was so despised, TC began to face a different kind of battle from those he had weathered on moving to Wales. Now he faced external battles. Local towns and villages didn't want Methodism. They could not stop local Methodists meeting as a society in private houses or barns but whenever the believers tried to buy a plot of land in order to erect a chapel building, they would usually be refused, because no one wanted a Methodist chapel in their village. A building was necessary in many places in order to hold the large numbers that were now gathering in the societies. But only five of the societies of Merioneth had managed to build a chapel by the time TC came to Bala.

Another great disadvantage was the fact that only ordained clergymen, that is, ministers in the Church of England, were allowed to conduct communion services, and before TC's coming there was no Methodist clergyman in the whole of North Wales. Communion services for these Methodists were very, very rare and only possible when a clergyman sympathetic to Methodism, on a preaching tour from the south, was passing through an area which had a Methodist chapel.

But now things were very different. At Bala there was a fairly large building and an ordained minister. TC held monthly communion services in the town and these attracted huge congregations. Very many people were converted in the meetings. By 1785, the Bala society had over 400 members and the congregation consisted of about two thousand people.

In effect, Bala became the centre for Methodism in North Wales. Up to that time, everybody had been travelling down to Llangeitho in Cardiganshire to attend a communion service, but now, they had an able leader in the north. As we have seen, as well as continually travelling to preach, TC also worked with children and young people. He would ride on horseback throughout North Wales, helping existing causes, planting new ones, and all without pay.

Dolgellau

One of the closest towns to Bala was Dolgellau. Surrounded by rugged mountains, this was an important location for trade and a key place to plant a church. Within a year of leaving the Church of England TC set his sights

Preaching on Bala Green during a Calvinistic Methodist Association

on sharing the gospel with the people of this town. He was to meet with fierce persecution when he tried. The locals could be as rugged as the surrounding mountains. He attempted to preach in the open air, but attracted a mob with hands full of rocks, before he had really got started!

TC recorded what happened:

> *I remember that I was in that district preaching in the open air, when I perceived a number of* [troublemakers] *drawing near to where I stood, armed with clods of stones, which they were about to hurl at me. A tall, well-built man stepped forward and stood between me and the danger, and told me to proceed without fear with what I had to tell the people.*

Thankfully, someone was brave enough to stand up between TC and the mob, and so he could get on and preach his sermon. One of his biographers commented: 'This stilled the enemy and the avenger, and the service passed off without a scene'. But this wasn't the best way to carry on. Open-air preaching was going to cause trouble. They needed to find a way to move inside, away from the rocks. So TC started looking for a building where they could meet as a church.

In those days, you couldn't just hold religious services in any building. You needed legal permission – a licence. TC found a house that was licensed, and so it looked as if the work could finally get going. He raised the money to demolish the building on the site so as to erect a new chapel. It was described as 'a most unsightly building.' It had no proper flooring, just bare earth, and the only seating was long benches with no backs.

The congregation grew, furniture was added, and a balcony installed. TC looked after the church and made sure it grew from strength to strength. Within twenty years they had outgrown the building. They looked for more land to build on. But again, it was the same old story. No one would sell them a suitable plot. Or, just to be spiteful, they would raise the price of the land until it was above what they could afford. The situation got so bad that, eventually, a friend had to buy the land on their behalf.

The story of how this was done is a good example of how TC's friends in England used to help him out. A Christian gentleman from London, T. C. Pugh, following the advice of TC, had decided to set up a business in Dolgellau. He succeeded so well that he became very familiar with many of the nobility of Dolgellau. When a suitable plot came on the market, Pugh went to the auction at the local pub. Everyone thought he was interested in buying the land for himself. But it was still not guaranteed that he would be successful.

Two things happened to make the land his. Firstly, there was a prayer meeting. Everything that the Methodists did was soaked in prayer. Later, we will see exactly how powerful prayer was in TC's life. Secondly, there was a dog fight. What occurred was that the auctioneer had registered Pugh's bid of £250 and said that if no one else put in a higher bid within the next ten minutes, the plot would be his. Just then some dogs, brought into the pub by their masters, began a fight. Everyone forgot about the bid! Ten minutes later, the sale was over and the land purchased.

With a glint in his eye, Pugh stood up and declared, 'There's the land for the Methodists to build their chapel'. People couldn't believe it. One man shouted out, 'Had I known that, I would have raised the bid by a hundred pounds'. This was typical of the attitude of so many to the work of the gospel. There was opposition everywhere. But this never deterred TC.

In one letter he gave a young minister the following advice: *The gospel can succeed nowhere without opposition, because it proclaims war first against all the kingdom of darkness. You must count the cost, labour to be faithful, and leave the issue with the Lord.* That is what he did in Dolgellau. It was this philosophy of ministry that kept him going, even in the most difficult and dangerous of places.

Corwen

Dolgellau was not the only place where TC and the Methodists faced opposition and persecution. Just up the road, was a town called Corwen. This is where TC met with 'the greatest danger to life and limb'. No one had been able to get a spiritual foothold in the town. The locals were closed to the gospel, and it was not possible to establish a work there until 1790.

This came about when a saddler named John Cadwaladr moved to the area. He decided to step out in faith and hold a meeting in his house. So he invited TC over from Bala to preach. You would think that people would let folk get on with their own lives, to do their own thing. But that was not to be. Word got out about the meeting and the local blacksmith was dispatched to threaten the visiting preacher.

The name of the blacksmith was David Hughes and he was often hired out to cause trouble. He knew what he was doing. He got hold of a big drum and began to bang it as loud as he could. This echoed down the valley and worked as a call to get the locals together. They hurried to the spot from all parts of the town and gathered as a mob outside the house.

Such a large crowd brought together by the banging of a drum, all shouting and swearing, must have been quite terrifying. The threats being made would have made the strongest faint with fear. The mob was shouting that TC had to leave the house. If he didn't they would pull the house down. TC realized that he had to leave. He really had no choice.

As he was leaving, the mob went mad and started throwing stones. Their threats had not been empty words. They meant business. And one stone hit TC square on the face and broke some of his teeth. He was covered in blood and had to run for his life. Nevertheless, he persevered, returning to the town some weeks later and eventually being given a hearing. A regular monthly meeting was established.

But there was still a cost to pay in the meantime. A believer, a local tenant called Richard White, opened his home for the monthly meetings. His rented farmhouse was called Bodhaulog. The opposition was still fierce. Not now in the form of lost teeth, but in the possibility of a lost tenancy. White's landlord gave him an ultimatum: unless he stopped welcoming the Methodists, he would be kicked out.

White's response was simple yet strong, 'Well, therefore, no more Bodhaulog for me'. He went on to buy *The Harp*, a closed-down inn, and converted the upper room into a meeting place. This was used as the main place of worship by the Methodists until a huge church building was opened for them. It was much bigger than their requirements, but TC was recorded as saying, *We did it in faith.*

TC was willing to battle. Why? What was he doing? He was bringing people the word of God. It was said of him:

> *The salvation of souls and the bringing of them into the possession of the highest treasures that man can possess, became the overwhelming passion of his life. This is what sustained him in the face of opposition and caused him to labour above what nature could endure.*

Physical health battles

TC seemed to have unlimited energy. Writing, printing, preaching, travelling back and forth to London, planting churches, holding huge communion services, riding over dangerous mountains, and being pelted with rocks, was there nothing that could stop him or slow him down? It seems that the lessons he had learnt in perseverance and trust in God as a young man had set him up for life. He was running a cross-country ultra-marathon as if it was a sprint on an indoor track.

Once, when about to cross the river Mersey to get to Liverpool, he remembered that he had left his money behind. He therefore left the boat he was on and went to retrieve his saddle-bag. By the time he returned, the boat had departed. A few minutes later it disappeared under the water and everyone on board was drowned. Travelling was both demanding and dangerous. But onwards he went.

TC was constantly journeying around North Wales and facing weather that would make even a Gore-Tex-clad mountaineer reconsider his journey. Yet, on he went. 'It was no small thing for him to ride, soaked to the skin, along remote mountainous paths, to find lodging in a tumbledown cottage'. In 1799, however, everything changed.

The winter of 1799 was particularly severe. TC had been away in Caernarfon and was returning home over the Migneint Mountain, between Caernarfon and Bala. Today this is a Special Area of Conservation and is part of one of the largest bogs in Wales. You wouldn't want to be there in the middle of winter with snow on the ground. This is exactly where TC found himself. And it nearly killed him.

Sitting on his horse, as the wind kept howling around him, he had no option but to hold on tightly to the reins, hoping to get home before the weather got any worse. But the biting wind that kept blowing on his exposed hands proved his downfall. He got frostbite in his left thumb. This would not be very dangerous today with easy access to hospitals and medication but two hundred years ago it was critical. The result of the frostbite was an infection that nearly ended his life. He came very close to death.

The truth that kept him going

During his illness the intense pain in his thumb brought him very low. What was going to happen? Was this going to be the end of his ministry? Or even of his life?

TC often repeated the advice that his good friend, John Evans, his fellow-elder in the Bala society, gave him at this time. On one occasion, John Evans had found him very downcast. TC asked him, 'John Evans, what do you think the Lord will do with me this time?' Evans came back quick as a flash, 'Indeed, I do not know what he will do with you; but this I know, Sir, he will do you no wrong.'

This underlying belief in the goodness of God, even in the face of trials, was one of the main reasons for TC's ability to keep going. He would urge others to believe the same, *Let us not be impatient and complain of our particular situations: but be our situation what it may, let us look up to that God, who can cause all things to work for our good.* Every Christian, even you, can believe that and we can all build our lives on it.

At one point the doctors simply looked at TC and shook their heads. The thumb had to be amputated or the infection would kill him. However, something miraculous happened. On the night before the thumb was amputated, there was a prayer meeting for him in Bala. His friends got together and started begging God to save him. This meeting was going to change everything for TC.

The room was full and the prayers were filled with urgency. Among the heart-felt pleas, an old man called Richard Owen got up and prayed the following words: 'Fifteen, Lord; wilt thou not give him to us for fifteen years?' He kept repeating the prayer, until, 'the earnest simplicity of the prayer thrilled the people'. There was a general conviction that the prayer would certainly be answered. Amazingly, TC recovered from his illness. But, make a note of the year – 1799.

TC accepted that he would encounter dangers and trials of one kind or another. He was living in the light of this. In a letter to a friend he wrote,

Plaque commemorating Thomas Charles and Mary Jones

I have but one desire, that of spending and being spent, till the good Lord, in infinite mercy, takes me to himself. And that is what he did. He just kept on going, no matter what the barrier or the battle. He showed the same attitude when he wrote: *Slothfulness in the service of God is as damning a sin as open rebellion against him.*

His strength never fully recovered after this severe illness. But he didn't give up. He would rather be a servant than a sloth. Unable to travel as much as before, he decided to turn his attention to the press. He devoted himself more to writing, and the consequences of this decision have had a huge impact on Wales. In fact, many would judge that the next fifteen years were 'the most fruitful of his life.'

Just as he expected opposition, TC also anticipated blessing. In a letter to Sally in 1783, before they were married, he emphasized the truth that storms and clouds are necessary, for, unless we have a cloud, we will never have rain. He believed that the clouds of opposition were signs that showers of blessings were on their way.

That shower of blessing was going to be glorious!

Chapter 5: Blessings

I love sunrises and sunsets. They are some of the most beautiful sights in the world. Watching the sunrise from the top of the Sugarloaf in Abergavenny, or the glowing red sunset from the seafront in Aberystwyth, is both awe-inspiring and soul-searching. Who made this happen? Do they know about me? Care about me?

TC must have seen many amazing sunrises and sunsets on his journeys. In fact, as we will see later, he wrote about his experiences of looking at the sun. At those moments, he may have pondered the words of David in Psalm 8 who, on viewing the sky, asked: 'What is man that you are aware of him, and the son of man that you care for him?' But TC was also reminded, when looking at the sky, that not only was the sun shining on him, but the Son was shining on him as well.

In this chapter we are going to see how TC believed in and experienced the blessings of God. In the midst of battles, organizing schools, and writing books, TC saw something of God that is both amazing and available to all believers, including you. Let's rewind a little to explore what I mean.

In his book *Heroes*, Iain H. Murray sums up what we have learnt about the work in Bala so far: 'the spread of the gospel in North Wales was not without much hard work and organization but the main emphasis was always upon prayerful dependence upon God.' While it has been good in this book to see TC's skills of organisation and his bravery in the face of opposition, we need to remember that he was a man of prayer. The following events can only have come about by the grace of God.

Dolgellau

I wonder what you thought happened to the church in Dolgellau? It was such a tough church to plant, and the people were nowhere near as open to the good news about Jesus Christ as the folk in Bala. Surely the church in

Bala would grow faster than the work in Dolgellau? Yet, in 1787, something amazing happened. Listen to TC describe it in a letter to a friend who had contributed towards erecting the church building in the town:

> *It seems, as if the face of the Lord was towards the place: in building the chapel the Lord has wonderfully assisted – far beyond expectation. It will be finished in a short time … in the mountainous country surrounding the little town the Gospel spreads powerfully, and those who never heard the sound of the Gospel till within these few years are brought by its power under the yoke of Christ. Indeed, it is wonderful to see and pleasing to think of the amazing change effected in different parts of this hitherto dark country, by its power only. The outpouring of the Spirit has been and still continues at times so abundant and powerful among those who made the utmost opposition to it.*

Revival had come! You may not know what a revival is. In some places people think it is a series of meetings where the Christian message is preached. But it is far, far more than that. Did you notice the words that TC used to describe the revival? – 'powerful', 'amazing', 'abundant', 'outpouring of the Spirit'. And what does it lead to? It brings a complete change of life. Folk are brought from darkness to light, from persecuting the church to praising the Head of the Church, Jesus Christ. That is a revival – an abundant outpouring of the Spirit upon an area, leading to complete changes of life.

Thomas Charles in later life

Four years later the revival would come to Bala.

Bala

Can you imagine people spilling out of a church building, walking down the road in the dark, crying and praying out loud? What if you went to school one day and half of your class had become Christians? How about learning that the boys who cause trouble at the end of your street had stopped swearing and drinking and were now going to prayer meetings instead? What would that be like? That is what happens in revival, and that is the kind of thing that happened in Bala.

TC describes one Sunday night in October 1791:

This glorious work began on a Sunday afternoon, in the chapel, where I preached twice that day, and cannot say, that there was anything particular in the ministry of that day, more than what I had often experienced among our people here. But, towards the close of the evening service, the Spirit of God seemed to work in a very powerful manner on the minds of great numbers present, who never appeared before to seek the Lord's face; but now, there was a general and a loud crying, 'What must I do to be saved,' and, 'God be merciful to me a sinner.' And, at about nine or ten o'clock at night, there was nothing to be heard from one end of the town to the other, but the cries and groans of people in distress of soul.

Throughout the following weeks there were prayer meetings every day. People were desperate to make sure that they were right with God, that they were saved. This is the key to understanding true revival and true faith. A genuine work of God will affect the heart. You won't just be moved by external things like music and large crowds, rather, you will experience the Spirit of God convicting you, calling you, and helping you cry out 'Abba Father'. You will understand and know that you are a child of God.

As letters poured in from around the world to ask for reports of the revival, TC responded as best he could. To one American pastor he wrote that many of those saved were *the most wild and abandoned that we had in the neighbourhood. I can hardly believe my eyes sometimes when I see in our chapel those, who were the most faithful servants of Satan, weeping, in the greatest distress, under a sense of sin and danger, and crying out for mercy.*

The revival came with such a shock that TC could call it a 'short work.' That is, 'there is little preparative work preceding. Convictions fly, like arrows from a strong well-bent bow.' He goes on to describe how people with absolutely no prior interest in the gospel were suddenly drawn in. One of the other things that stood out most to TC was the age of many of those affected by the outpouring of the Spirit. He was amazed by the work of God among the young people. The children who had learnt to read and write, then memorized the Bible, had seen their faith set aflame. Those who had never known the Lord were converted, and those who were Christians already were given a deeper experience of God. All knew the smile of God.

In a letter written to prove the authenticity of the revival, one of the evidences TC gives is, *in particular, among young people … no harps, but the golden harps which St. John speaks of, have been played upon in the neighbourhood.* Mentioning that there were 'no harps' seems like an odd thing to pick on, but we need to remember what the harp represented in those days.

Today, playing the harp is seen as something good and cultural. Usually it is regarded as a lovely part of the Welsh national identity. However, back in those days, the harp was more of a Flying V electric guitar: something that represented rebellion. It was the accompaniment and the encourager of drunkenness and of other sins that followed. TC even wrote a catechism that taught children not to get involved in festivals that included harps. Do you remember the question, 'Is dancing a sin?' The answer was, 'Yes'. Bible verses included, 'Woe unto them that rise up early in the morning, that they may follow strong drink … and the harp…'. The effect of the revival was such that there was no drunkenness and it was noted that 'the harpists were seen leaving the place in disappointment, cursing the "priest in the black cap", who had bewitched the people.' TC's letter was indicating how lives had been completely changed and hearts were full of praise to God.

In the New Testament letter of Ephesians, the Apostle Paul declares that God is 'able to do immeasurably more than all we ask or imagine, according to his power'. This is what was happening to TC. This was beyond belief. The revival started to spread out and went from community to community. TC wrote that this was a *dispensation so glorious, I never beheld, nor indeed expected to see in my day*. Further awakenings continued, and spread to other neighbourhoods over the next three years. As we saw at the start of this book, the Methodist Revival had been spreading and expanding for twenty years in a similar way before he was born. God was at work and he still is at work today.

Those across the border scoffed at the revival. They hadn't experienced one and so were very sceptical. Could God save hundreds at one time? Or was this just Welsh fantasy? TC was aware of this and wrote:

In England ... they would consider the whole as wild enthusiasm, and the effects of over-heated imagination; we deny not, but there may be dross mixed with the fine gold; but that this work is of God, we can no more doubt, than that light and heat proceed from the sun.

Not everyone in Wales embraced the revival. I wonder who you think didn't get involved? We know that young people got behind it; we also know that people who were living in darkness came to the light. One biographer tells us the sad truth 'while these religious awakenings were proceeding, most Welsh clergymen remained only as onlookers. This is something to be regretted'.

How shocking is that? The leaders of churches didn't get involved in the revival. They stayed away. There is a serious warning here. You can be in the church, even involved in the life of the church, but still miss out on God. Just because you go to church, doesn't mean you truly know and want to know God.

Dear reader, my greatest prayer is that you truly know God, and never miss out on his smile. You might be thinking that if there was a revival, you would never miss out. But how do you know? One of the ways you can know, is by thinking through how you respond to the smile of God now, today.

Blessings

Have you been wondering, what is the smile of God? Is it revival? Is it an experience during revival? Can I know it outside of revival times … today even? We most certainly see the smile of God in revival. But that is not the entire answer. If it were, we could only know his smile in times of awesome outpourings of the Spirit. But what about now? TC believed that you could see the shining face of God at all times. And this is something he desperately wanted, and encouraged others to desire as well.

Matthew Henry wrote a little sentence with a big impact: 'We need desire no more to make us happy, than to have God's face shine upon us, to have God love us, and let us know that he loves us'. For him, the smile of God was the face of God shining on us. What is that? It is simply knowing that God loves us. But that knowledge is not simply intellectual. For example, I might know that one TV celebrity loves another, or that my best friend loves his wife, but it doesn't change me. But to know that my wife loves me and to see her smile at me changes everything.

We all want to see a smile – especially the smile of God – and to know that we are loved. The amazing news of the Bible is that God wants to smile on us. God wants to bless us and to let us know he loves us. But, where exactly do we see the face of God? Is this some kind of mystical experience? No, not really. Where do we see the face of God? We see it in Christ. What did Jesus say in John 14? 'Don't you know me, Philip, even after I have been among you such a long time? Anyone who has seen me has seen the Father. How can you say, "Show us the Father"?' How about Colossians 1? 'The Son is the image of the invisible God, the firstborn over all creation.'

In Christ we see the face of God in blessing. Paul writes in 2 Corinthians 4:6, 'For God, who said, "Let light shine out of darkness", made his light shine in our hearts to give us the light of the knowledge of God's glory displayed in the face of Christ'. In a sense, Christ himself is the smile of God. It is all of grace. We see the smile of God at the cross of Calvary. This is how we know that we are loved. And that means his smile will never leave us as it is a smile based on the finished work of Christ, not on us.

TC believed that the Spirit would help us, even outside of revival times, to know this smile. He puts it so beautifully,

> *The rays of heavenly glory, issuing from Christ, pervade the inmost parts of the soul, and convey new vigour to the spiritual life.*

For TC, Christ is like the sun shining in all its brilliance. Indeed, elsewhere TC writes:

> *It is like looking on the midday sun in a clear summer's day. Our weak eyes are dazzled with its splendour, and unable to look any longer.*

It is clear from the writings and letters of TC that he sought God's blessing at all times. He was passionate about seeking Christ's face and realised that the knowledge of this could increase and decrease. He noted:

> *In proportion as the knowledge of the glory of God in the face of Jesus Christ shines in our hearts, so will our confidence and delight in him increase.*

In a sense, if you want to be blessed, you simply need to look to Jesus! That is where we see the smile of God.

The ultimate blessing

TC nearly died in 1799 but the prayers of the people and the power of God kept him alive. Just as was requested in prayer, he was given fifteen more years. During those years he saw more and more Bibles printed, books written, churches planted, and the Methodist Church[4] in Wales was settled and solidified. It was a fruitful time.

---

4   It was called 'The Calvinistic Methodist Church of Wales.' It was also known later as 'The Presbyterian Church of Wales', both names being legally valid.

How do you think TC felt about his ministry as he came to the end of his life? The year before he died he said: *I feel ashamed when I think how little I have done, compared with what I ought to have done – with what was wanted to be done.* How shocking is that! Surely he could see what he had done? Maybe he could but he knew that it was all the work of the Lord. In a sermon on *Spiritual Pride* he preached: *humility is the strength and ornament of all other graces; it is food that nourisheth them; the soil in which they grow.*

It seems to me that one of the reasons TC was able to keep going, no matter how many set-backs, oppositions, battles or pain he had to face, was this: he knew the danger of pride. He continued in the sermon: *It is our pride and self-sufficiency, and not our weakness, which gives any inward or outward enemy the victory over us.* TC gave up everything in order to remain in Wales, for better or for worse, and he gave his everything for the work of the gospel.

In 1813 he wrote to a friend, *I have been, for these two months past and more, in a state of great body debility; supposed by the doctors to be the effect of an over-exertion of body and mind.* Sadly, just a little time before, his dear wife had a stroke and was disabled as a result. He writes to another friend, *we are both on life's descent, but she appears to be travelling faster than I am.*

They visited the seaside town of Barmouth for some respite and preaching. Sitting in this lovely little Welsh haven, TC turned to his loving wife and said, *Well, Sally, the fifteen years is almost at an end.* As one biographer says, they were 'racing each other to the grave.' The last weeks were very difficult. TC was suffering; Sally was struggling; their eldest son was seriously ill, nearly dying; their long-serving maid contracted typhus fever and died in less than a fortnight.

This was indeed a time of being in a 'furnace'. But his 'soul was cheerful' even in the face of such pain and anguish. One Tuesday evening, as he was going to bed, he spoke tenderly to Sally, *Well, my dear, if I should die and leave you, the Lord still lives to take care of you.* TC had every trust in the Lord. The next day his health deteriorated and a friend said to him, 'Well, Mr Charles *bach*, the day of tribulation has come.' His response was confident, *There is a refuge*. With that, he spoke no more, his breath grew faint, and at around 10 pm on Wednesday, 5 October, he went to his eternal refuge.

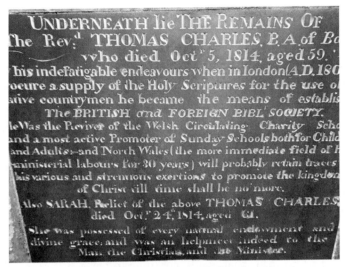

The gravestone in Llanycil churchyard

Conclusion

I love history. I did it at A-level and a lot of my degree focused on church history. But whenever I study someone from the past I always want to ask the question: 'So what?' I want to learn from history. As we come, then, to the end of this little book, I want to ask that question: 'So what?'

I have found researching and writing about the life of TC a real encouragement and challenge. It has been so helpful and inspiring to me as a Christian. I hope it has helped you too. I find it amazing what God did during one short life. As TC himself commented at a meeting in 1795,

> *Sixty years ago it would have been difficult to find a single family calling upon God in North Wales: but now, by the grace of heaven, there are hundreds of families worshipping God in every county.*

But TC had no idea what would continue to happen through the work of the Bible Society over the next two hundred years. By today, they supply Bibles to over two hundred countries! Just like the celebration that happened when the cart of Bibles was pulled down the main road in Bala, similar scenes are repeated around the world today. You can even watch a video of Bibles being delivered to the Kimyal community in West Papua after they had waited for them for forty-seven years![5]

As we come to the end of this book may I take a little more of your time and apply some things to our lives. Let me give you three pieces of advice that I think TC would write to young people today.

1. Believe

TC had a heart for people to come and to know the Lord Jesus personally. His own life had been transformed by meeting Jesus. Let's be clear, going to

---

5   https://youtu.be/ag2AzWgRKAk

church does not make you a Christian. Reading this book does not make you a Christian. A Christian is someone who has realized that he is sinful, even if they are studious and well-behaved like the young TC, but has understood that God sent his only Son, Jesus Christ, to die for us on the cross. His death can be our death. That is, our punishment can be poured out on him. He can be our substitute. But we must believe and receive this. Have you done so?

2. Battle on

TC knew what it was to face battles and we should too. Jesus said in John 16 that in this world we would have struggles. TC was clear on this: *The gospel can succeed nowhere without opposition ... you must count the cost.* In doing so, you will need to say with TC: *I have but one desire, that of spending and being spent, till the good Lord in infinite mercy, takes me to himself.* For many of us, this will involve keeping going, even when there seems to be little fruit.

I love the way that TC spoke about his love for Wales: *For better or for worse.* Don't give up. After waiting for years, TC could finally write in a letter to a friend about,

> *a dispensation so glorious, I never beheld, not indeed expected to see in my day. In (the) course of the 8 years I (have) laboured in this country, I have had frequent opportunities of seeing, and feeling also, much of the divine presence in the Lord's work and ordinances, and great success attending the ministration of the word; but nothing to equal the present work...*

How was TC able to wait for this, even when he couldn't find a church and had to work behind the shop counter? He simply saw himself as a sponge. In a letter written in 1799, he said that he was a dry sponge and that everything he had to give when he was squeezed was given of God. This is what is meant by the word 'grace'. He goes on to explore that gift: *God does not give us half but a whole Christ. Let our faith be as large in receiving as his heart is in giving.*

I'm sure that TC would not have wanted us to look at him. My hunch is that he would ultimately say: 'Look to Christ!' So, my final piece of advice from the life of TC must simply be:

3. Behold!

In steering Christians away from pride, TC described the humble life: *Not only is the foundation laid in mere grace, but the top-stone will be brought forth with shouting, 'Grace, grace!'* TC emphasized, again and again, that we must have deeper views of Christ. We are continually to look to him. He uses the word 'proportion' a lot.

> *The effect is always proportioned to its cause, so the clearer our comprehension of, and the more firm our belief is, in God's love towards us, the more ardent will be our love to him, and the more active our diligence in his service.*

The more we see Jesus, the more we will love him. The more we love him, the more we will live for him. This isn't just an intellectual pursuit of the historical Jesus. This is a passionate exploration of the Christ who reigns on high today. As such we end up being overwhelmed by his love. Look to Jesus. Increase the proportion. As TC wrote in an essay:

> *In the face or person of Christ alone, can we see the glory of God and of all divine perfections. When we see his glory as held forth in the gospel, we see the glory and image of God. And by this believing sight, we are changed into the same image.*

Simply put: 'It is impossible to grow in grace, without growing in the true knowledge of Jesus Christ.' That is why TC was so passionate to get people into the Bible. For that is where they would see Jesus.

This is TC's desire for us all:

> *May you find him whom your soul loveth, and be continually happy in the manifestation and enjoyment of his love. To know him is life eternal; to feel his love shed abroad in the heart, is heaven.*

Thomas Charles' statue outside Tegid Chapel, Bala

Further Reading
(in order of size and depth of content)

Gwyn Davies, *A Light in the Land, Christianity in Wales: 200-2000* (Bridgend: Bryntirion Press, 2002).

Iain H. Murray, *Heroes* (Edinburgh: Banner of Truth Trust, 2009).

William Williams, *Welsh Calvinistic Methodism* (1872; reprinted Bridgend: Bryntirion Press, 1998).

John Morgan Jones and William Morgan (trans. by John Aaron), *The Calvinistic Methodist Fathers of Wales* (Edinburgh: Banner of Truth, 2008).

Thomas Charles' Spiritual Counsels (1836; reprinted Edinburgh: Banner of Truth, 1993).

John Aaron, *Thomas Charles of Bala* (Edinburgh: Banner of Truth Trust, 2021).

D. E. Jenkins, *The Rev. Thomas Charles of Bala*, 3 volumes (Denbigh: Llewelyn Jenkins, 1908).